UNCONVENTIONAL
SCIENCE

TURNING POOP
INTO POWER

BY ALEXIS BURLING

CONTENT CONSULTANT
Bo Hu, PhD
Associate Professor, Department of Bioproducts and
Biosystems Engineering, University of Minnesota

Core Library

An Imprint of Abdo Publishing
abdobooks.com

Cover image: Some farmers turn their cows' manure
into energy.

abdocorelibrary.com

Published by Abdo Publishing, a division of ABDO, PO Box 398166,
Minneapolis, Minnesota 55439. Copyright © 2020 by Abdo Consulting
Group, Inc. International copyrights reserved in all countries. No part of this
book may be reproduced in any form without written permission from the
publisher. Core Library™ is a trademark and logo of Abdo Publishing.

Printed in the United States of America, North Mankato, Minnesota
022019
092019

THIS BOOK CONTAINS
RECYCLED MATERIALS

Cover Photo: Rudmer Zwerver/Shutterstock Images
Interior Photos: Rudmer Zwerver/Shutterstock Images, 1; Joerg Boethling/Alamy, 4–5; Mark
Boulton/Alamy, 7; Red Line Editorial, 9; Bettmann/Getty Images, 12–13; iStockphoto, 17, 18–19,
20 (cow), 20 (pellets), 20 (energy company), 22–23; Jo Havel/iStockphoto, 20 (fertilizer); Volodymyr
Kotoshchuk/iStockphoto, 20 (house); Jay Directo/AFP/Getty Images, 26–27; Ted S. Warren/
AP Images, 29, 43; Tsering Topgyal/AP Images, 32; Ben Birchall/PA Wire URN:24863433/Press
Association/AP Images, 34–35, 45; Josh Reynolds/AP Images, 37; Randy Duchaine/Alamy, 38

Editor: Marie Pearson
Series Designer: Ryan Gale

Library of Congress Control Number: 2018966011

Publisher's Cataloging-in-Publication Data

Names: Burling, Alexis, author.
Title: Turning poop into power / by Alexis Burling.
Description: Minneapolis, Minnesota : Abdo Publishing, 2020 | Series: Unconventional science |
    Includes online resources and index.
Identifiers: ISBN 9781532119019 (lib. bdg.) | ISBN 9781532173196 (ebook) | ISBN
    9781644940921 (pbk.)
Subjects: LCSH: Waste products as fuel--Juvenile literature. | Organic waste as fuel--Juvenile
    literature. | Biogas--Juvenile literature. | Environmental protection--Juvenile literature.
    | Energy source development--Juvenile literature. | Alternative energy sources--
    Juvenile literature. | Sustainable energy sources--Juvenile literature.
Classification: DDC 665.776--dc23

CONTENTS

CHAPTER ONE

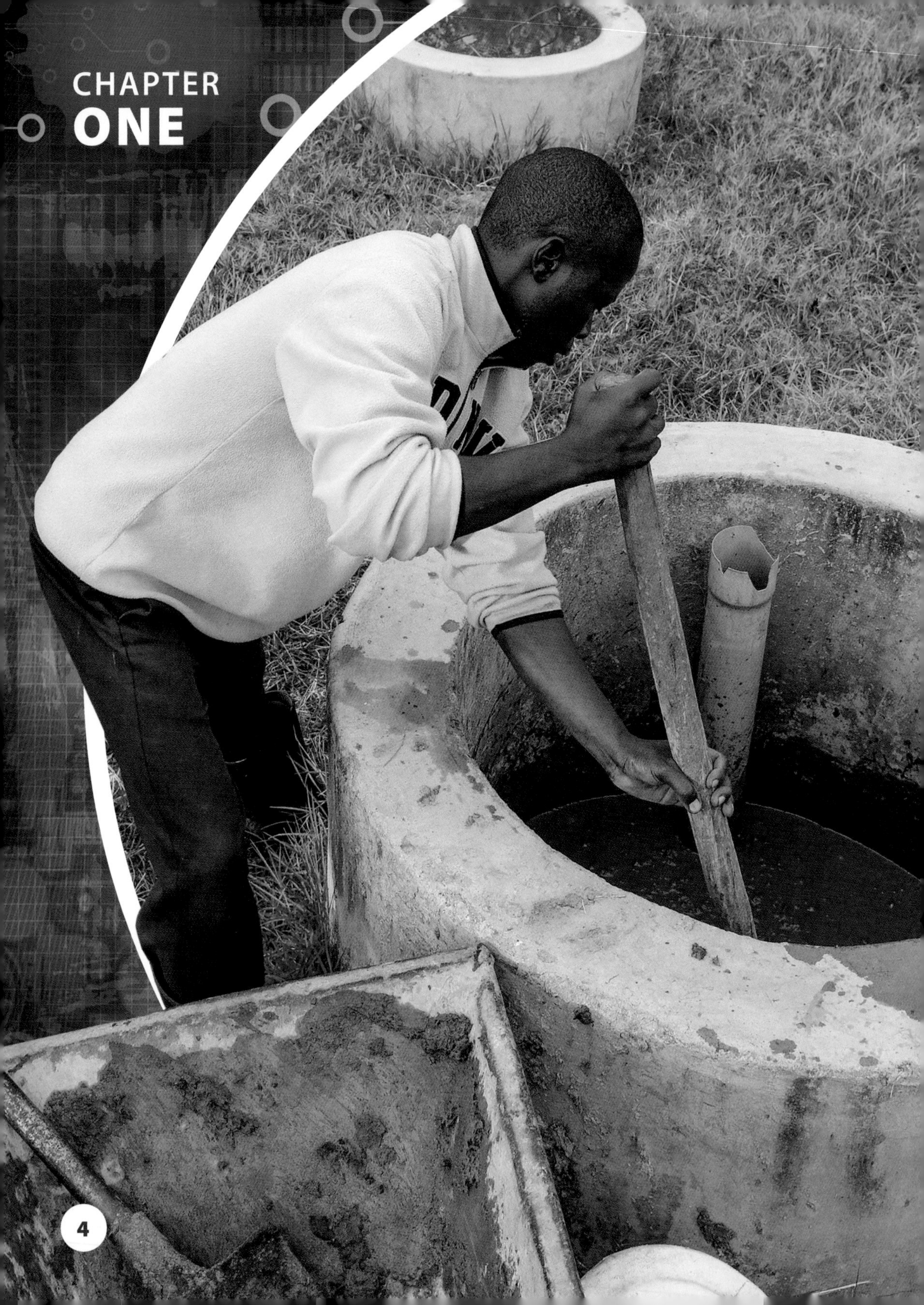

POOP: A SMELLY SOLUTION

Leroy Mwasaru lives in Kenya, Africa. When he was in high school in 2012, his school needed a new building. Workers started building it. But then there was a problem.

The dorm was being built on a location that had pit-style toilets. Tractors started digging. Sewage, or organic waste, leaked into a nearby stream. It was the only source of drinking water for Leroy's community. Now the stream was contaminated.

Many places in Kenya use bioreactors as a way to reuse human and animal waste.

There were other problems at Leroy's school too. The cafeteria staff used firewood to heat food. The smoke burned everyone's eyes. It was hard to breathe. Plus, the need for wood was shrinking the village's forests.

Over the next four years, Leroy and four friends worked on a solution. They hoped it would fix both problems at once. Their idea was to use human waste for fuel. In 2016, the students designed a model of a human waste bioreactor. A bioreactor is a machine in which a biological process

DEFORESTATION IN EAST AFRICA

East Africa has many different types of forests. Fifteen percent of the wildlife population along the coast is found nowhere else in the world. But these woods are in danger. According to the World Wildlife Fund, East Africa lost around 15 million acres (6 million ha) of forest between 2000 and 2012. Much of this loss was because East Africans collected too much timber for fuel. The region could lose 30 million acres (12 million ha) between 2010 and 2030 if current practices continue.

Bioreactors can turn human waste into fuel for cooking.

happens. It had an underground chamber that held raw sewage and kitchen scraps. Microorganisms in the sludge broke down the waste and turned it into power.

With one invention, Leroy improved the lives of people in his community. Because of his efforts, the school saved 3.92 million Kenyan schillings in natural

LEROY MWASARU GOES NATIONAL

Leroy's invention attracted global attention. But the budding scientist didn't stop there. After he graduated from high school, he formed Greenpact. The company makes affordable bioreactors. It sells them to companies and families throughout Kenya. In 2018, *Forbes* magazine made a list of the top 30 African businesspeople under 30 years old. Leroy was the youngest person on the list. Greenpact has also turned Leroy into a millionaire.

gas costs over two years. That's approximately $39,000. He and his friends also helped transform the way people around the world thought about energy.

FROM POOP TO POWER

Doing anything with poop besides flushing it down the toilet can seem a little gross. But the truth is that poop is very useful. It is a biomass. That's the name for all living or recently living materials that can be used to make energy.

Similar to wood, poop is a renewable source of energy. That means it can be produced over and

BIOGAS REACTORS

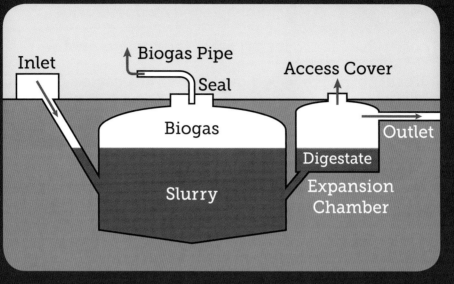

Inlet

Biogas Pipe

Seal

Access Cover

Biogas

Outlet

Digestate

Slurry

Expansion Chamber

A biogas reactor is an airtight tank where poop and other organic waste can be broken down and used for energy. A mixture of methane and carbon dioxide forms in the slurry. The gas rises to the top of the tank. There, it is collected for later use. The slurry becomes digestate. This substance is high in nutrients. It can be used to fertilize plants. Why do you think the gas rises?

over again. It takes renewable energy sources only a few months or years to become fuel. This makes them more sustainable.

The science behind the poop-to-power process is simple. Poop and other biomass are collected in an airtight tank. Microorganisms in the sludge gobble it down. The organisms make biogas during digestion.

The biogas is usually methane and carbon dioxide. These gases are collected and used for energy. The leftover solids are called digestate. They can be used as crop fertilizer.

A GLOBAL SOLUTION

For thousands of years, humans have relied on fossil fuels for energy. Some examples of fossil fuels are coal, oil, and natural gas. These fossil fuels come from underground deposits of decayed plants and animals. They take millions of years to form. Today, companies drill or mine for these energy sources. The energy is used to fuel cars and light homes.

But burning these fossil fuels is bad for the environment. It is the largest human source of carbon dioxide emissions. Emissions are the production and discharge of something such as a gas. Too much carbon dioxide in the atmosphere causes global warming. Usually some of the sun's heat reflects back into space. But carbon dioxide traps some of that heat. Since the 1800s, Earth's average temperature has risen approximately 1.62 degrees Fahrenheit (0.9°C).

People like Leroy are working to combat that problem. Poop might be stinky. It definitely looks disgusting. But it could be the key to creating sustainable energy resources for the future.

EXPLORE ONLINE

Chapter One describes a teenager's quest to turn poop into power in order to solve a problem at his school. The video below is an interview with Leroy Mwasaru. He talks about his inspiration for the project. He also describes obstacles he faced along the way. What new information did you learn from this interview?

CHANGEMAKER: LEROY MWASARU
abdocorelibrary.com/poop-into-power

Gathering Chi

POOP THROUGH THE AGES

Leroy found a way to convert poop into energy. But his idea wasn't a new one. For thousands of years, people all over the world have been using poop for power.

In 6000 BCE, the ancient Egyptians found a use for manure, or animal poop. They used the waste to fertilize their crops. Manure contains a lot of nutrients. The nitrogen, phosphorous, and potassium in the poop helps plants grow.

The Egyptians also used poop for heat. Burning wood was too expensive.

Settlers on the Great Plains in the United States burned bison poop for fuel.

There weren't a lot of trees in the desert. Egyptians used poop instead. First, they mushed the poop into log-shaped patties. Then they put the logs in the sun to dry. Burning the dried logs provided a cheap source of heat and light.

Using poop for fuel was a common practice in other civilizations too. In the 1200s CE, the Chinese kept their sewage tanks covered. The waste inside broke down. The sludge released biogas. The biogas was collected and converted into power.

ANCIENT INCAN POOP

The Inca Empire was one of the greatest civilizations in history. A key to the Inca's success was animal dung. The Inca lived in the Andes Mountains in Peru during the 1400s and 1500s. Normally, crops can't grow in high places. But the Inca used llama dung to fertilize the soil. It made growing corn possible. The Inca also used poop as cooking fuel and as a glue to make pottery.

GONG FARMERS

In the 1400s, handling poop became a whole different matter.

In England, it was someone's job to collect human waste from homes. Many young boys were hired for the job. They were paid a lot of money.

At the time, most people used outhouses behind their homes. Underneath these bathrooms were giant pits. The pits were called gongs. When the gongs were full, someone had to jump inside to shovel out the poop. These poop collectors were called *gongfermors*, or gong farmers.

Because of the stench, gong farmers worked at night. The poop they collected was called "night soil."

BUFFALO CHIPS

During the 1800s in the United States, people left the East Coast to find new land in the West. Many settled in the middle of the country in an area called the Great Plains. The fields were flat. There weren't many trees. Settlers had to find other sources of fuel. Bison roamed the land. Settlers used bison poop dried by the sun. Bison were also called buffalos. The hard patties were called "buffalo chips." They were lit on fire. The burning chips produced heat and fuel for cooking.

Most of it was dumped into the Thames River. But some of the poop was delivered to nearby farms. Many farms used human waste in addition to animal manure for fertilizer.

MODERN PIT TOILETS

Gong farmers had jobs in cities around the world until the 1800s. Some even worked in New York City. Today, flushing toilets are common in many places. So are sewers that transport human waste to treatment centers.

But many people today also use special toilets called composting toilets. There are different types. Some, like those used at campgrounds, are basic. Some others in homes are more complicated.

One basic design uses two pits next to each other. The first pit has a small amount of twigs, leaves, and other agricultural waste inside. It sits underneath a moveable toilet. The other pit is empty. When the first pit gets full of human waste, the toilet is moved to

When people use a composting toilet, they must add organic matter such as sawdust afterward to help the waste break down.

the empty pit. The full pit is covered. Microorganisms break down the sludge in the pit. The sludge becomes fertilizer called compost.

In some cases, this system is only used to fertilize crops. But many farmers around the world have also started to harness the biogas. They use it to power their buildings and barns. People have used poop for thousands of years. But figuring out how to do so on a massive scale is the wave of the future.

CHAPTER THREE

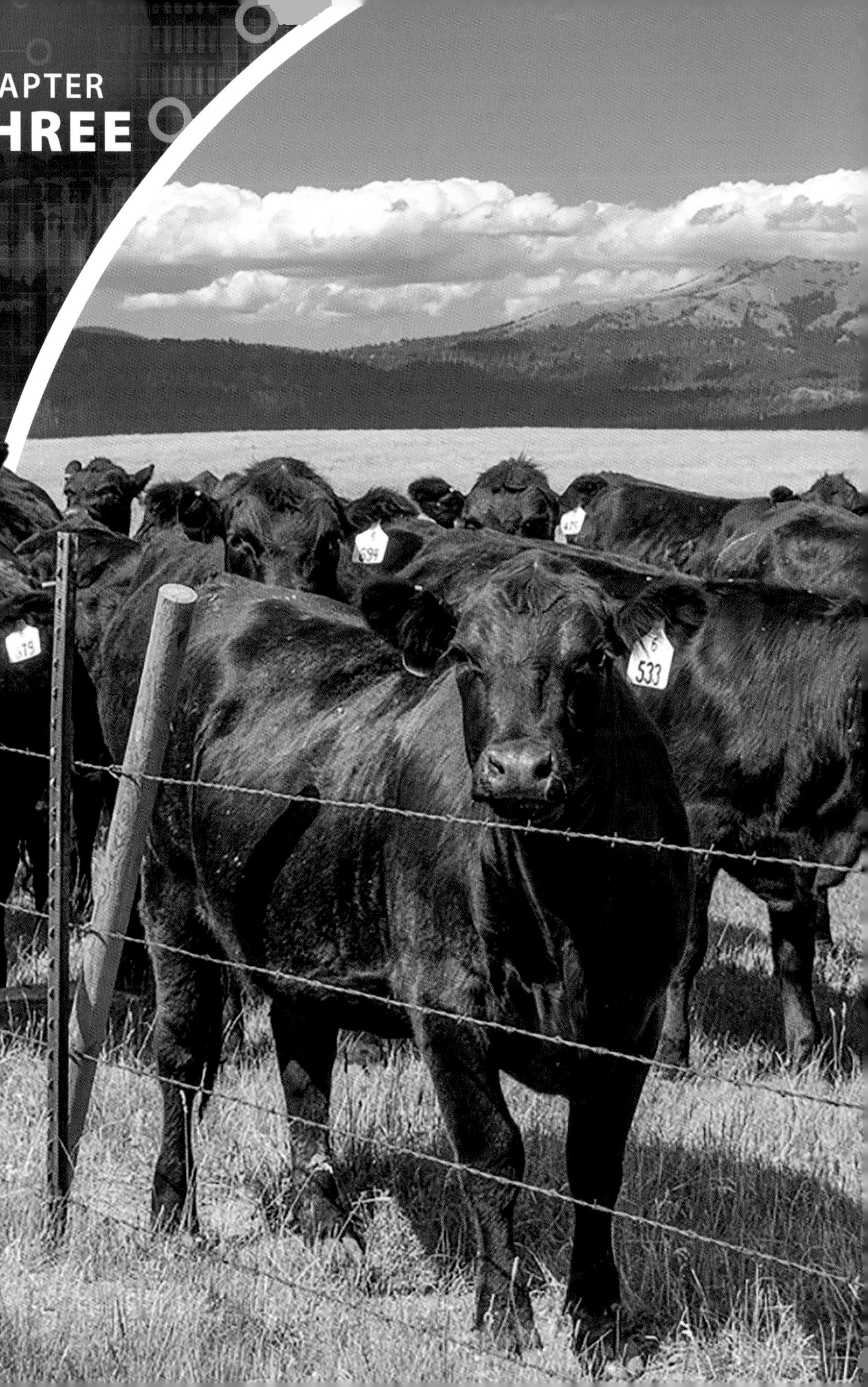

DUNG DIGESTERS

Farm animals are cute. But they are also a major source of poop. There are approximately 60,000 dairy farms in the United States. Most farms have an average of 135 cows. A 1,000-pound (450 kg) dairy cow produces an average of 80 pounds (35 kg) of manure each day.

Too much animal waste on the ground can cause problems. Nitrogen is a nutrient in poop. It seeps into groundwater, draining into lakes and rivers. There, it can cause algal blooms. The algae suffocate fish. Manure also releases

Cattle produce a lot of manure. Digesters are one way of dealing with that manure.

ANAEROBIC DIGESTER PRODUCTS

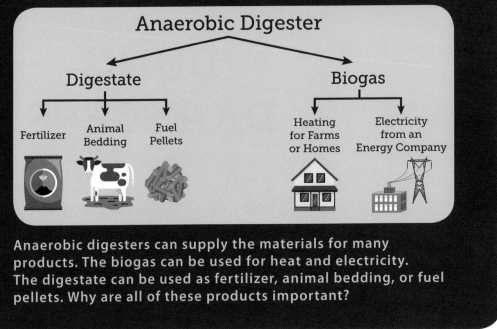

Anaerobic Digester

Digestate

- Fertilizer
- Animal Bedding
- Fuel Pellets

Biogas

- Heating for Farms or Homes
- Electricity from an Energy Company

Anaerobic digesters can supply the materials for many products. The biogas can be used for heat and electricity. The digestate can be used as fertilizer, animal bedding, or fuel pellets. Why are all of these products important?

methane, a greenhouse gas. Farm animal manure causes 14.5 percent of annual global greenhouse gas emissions.

But scientists are working with farmers to solve the issue. The US Environmental Protection Agency set up a program. It builds anaerobic digesters on US farms. An anaerobic digester is a large machine that acts like a stomach. It uses bacteria to break down poop to make biogas. The biogas is then burned to produce power. The digester keeps oxygen gas out. It works almost exactly like Leroy Mwasaru's model. But everything happens on a larger scale.

TYPES OF DIGESTERS

There are many types of anaerobic digesters. But three of the most common are plug flow digesters, complete mix digesters, and covered lagoons. Plug flow digesters are also called tubular or balloon digesters. These long, narrow tanks are often below ground. They have an opening on each end. Waste enters one end. As more waste is added, it pushes its way down the tank. Most have a

BIOGAS LEADERS

Countries including Germany and China are leaders in using biogas as a renewable energy source. In Germany, there are approximately 8,000 plants. They process animal and agricultural waste for power. These plants use gas for heat and to make natural gas. Biogas provides 4.6 percent of Germany's electricity. China uses biogas for 10 percent of its total natural gas. In rural areas, more than 42 million homes with farm animals have backyard anaerobic digesters that process poop to make fuel for cooking.

Some farms use complete mix digesters.

plastic or rubber cover. As the biogas rises, it flows out through a pipe on top.

A complete mix digester can be above or below ground. It is a heated, sealed tank. This digester uses a motor or pump to mix the poop and push it through a tube on the other side. Sometimes water or liquid waste is also added to the slurry. The biogas rises to the top of the tank. Then it is collected.

The third most popular anaerobic digester is the covered lagoon. These are mostly used on pig farms.

Mushy manure gets poured into pits in the ground. As the biogas rises, it gets trapped underneath a floating cover. Then the gas is collected. Covered lagoon digesters are only used in warmer climates. They are the smelliest digesters of all.

A FOUL SIDE EFFECT

There are more than 253 working anaerobic digesters on US farms. In 2017, these digesters reduced greenhouse gas emissions by 4.35 million short tons (3.95 million metric tons). They also created approximately 1.08 million megawatt-hours of electricity.

But some farms or treatment plants that process waste for farms are getting negative feedback. People in the surrounding communities say the air smells awful. One of the main goals of anaerobic digesters is to remove bad odors from the environment. But if the machines aren't working properly, the stinky smell will leak into the air.

Many farms build digesters but later shut them down. Perhaps the biggest reason digesters on farms shut down is cost. Often, they cost more to run than what farmers save on energy.

The debate continues over what to do about animal poop. But scientists seem mostly unified about another subject: toilets for humans. In fact, there are a lot of exciting developments on turning human waste into power.

FURTHER EVIDENCE

Chapter Three has quite a bit of information about anaerobic digestion. What is one of the main points of this chapter? What key evidence supports this point? Watch the video about anaerobic digestion at the website below. Does the information in the video support the main point of the chapter? Does it present new evidence?

MUCH A-DOO ABOUT POO

abdocorelibrary.com/poop-into-power

CHAPTER
FOUR

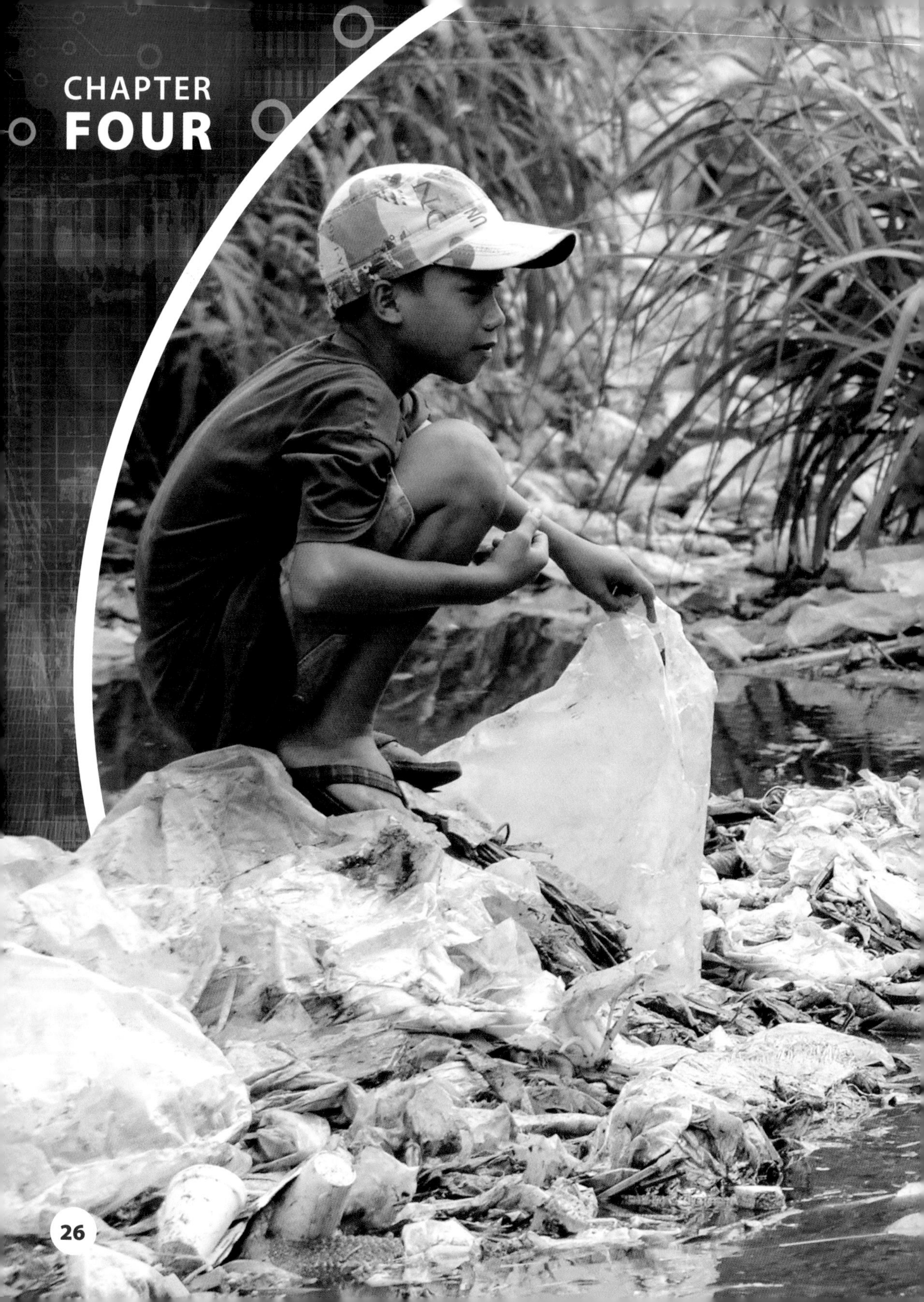

BATHROOM BREAKTHROUGHS

There is a world sanitation crisis. Approximately 60 percent of the global population is without access to a working bathroom at home. A lot of places also have contaminated water. Approximately 80 percent of wastewater worldwide flows back into the ground or rivers without being treated. As a result, 1.8 billion people drink water from a source that may contain feces, or poop.

People need clean water to drink and bathe in. More toilets and improved sanitation practices could prevent around 842,000 deaths each year. Finding new ways to get rid of poop responsibly could also produce heat, electricity,

Many people around the world do not have access to clean water.

WORLD TOILET DAY

In 2013, the UN General Assembly created World Toilet Day. Every year on November 19, the UN works with governments and organizations worldwide. They educate people about toilets and sanitation. Each year, there is a different subject. In 2017, the theme was wastewater. The UN made a video about where poop goes after it leaves the body. The video also describes how waste could be transformed into energy.

and natural gas for millions of people.

REINVENT THE TOILET CHALLENGE

In 2011, the Bill and Melinda Gates Foundation announced the Reinvent the Toilet Challenge. It was a national contest to see who could design the best toilet. The winning teams would receive a cash prize.

The rules were simple. The toilet could not depend on any sewer, electricity, or water source to work. It had to get rid of germs. It also needed to create a reusable resource, such as power. Finally, contestants had to

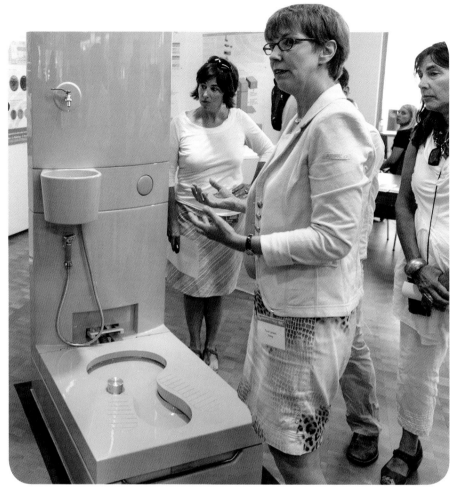

The Reinvent the Toilet Challenge inspired many people to invent new toilets.

design a toilet that would cost less than five cents per user per day.

A year later, the winner was announced. A team from California Institute of Technology (CalTech) won $100,000. They designed three types of toilets.

Each toilet had a tank underneath. The tank acted as a mini-anaerobic digester. It broke down the poop.

The toilets worked because they were connected to a solar panel outside. The panel took rays from the sun and converted them into power. That power was used to charge an electrochemical reactor. This machine uses electricity to drive the chemical reactions. The reactor sped up the anaerobic digestion process. Hydrogen gas rose to the top of the tank. It flowed into a holding tube. The gas could be stored for later use as energy. This way the toilet could be used at night.

A NEW TOILET CHALLENGE

After winning the first Reinvent the Toilet Challenge in 2012, the CalTech team built models to test in India and China. The toilets worked. But there was a bigger problem to consider. When parts break in developing countries, people may not know how to fix them. The team made sure the toilets came with spare parts. If something went wrong, sensors on the toilet sent a photo of the problem to a device. The photo showed people how to replace the broken part.

Water from the slurry was also separated into a different tank. It was sanitized and could be used for watering crops. The leftover digestate became crop fertilizer.

MORE POWERFUL TOILETS

As of 2018, the Reinvent the Toilet Challenge is still going strong. Many more teams have won money for developing new designs. A team from the University of Toronto created a toilet that burns the poop using ultraviolet light. A toilet from a university in the United Kingdom transforms feces into biological charcoal using a chemical process. The charcoal can be used as a fuel source or for fertilizer.

In 2016, the winning team created the Nano Membrane Toilet. A user flushes the toilet by hand by pushing down the seat cover. This triggers a system of moving gears on the side of the bowl. The gears cause the toilet bowl to rotate. A brush cleans the bowl as it moves. The poop falls into a tank below. The flush happens without using water or power. But the liquid

Biological charcoal is also called biochar.

waste is also collected from the toilet. It is cleaned. Then it can be used for watering plants.

In the modern age, toilet bowls come in many shapes and sizes. But in the near future, some might be able to power homes. In fact, scientists are already working on this and other fascinating inventions, like poop-powered buses, poop-powered smartphones, and more!

STRAIGHT TO THE
SOURCE

Bill Gates challenged people to invent a toilet that could turn poop into power. He described a visit to one of the factories in his blog:

> *I watched the piles of feces go up the conveyer belt and drop into a large bin. They made their way through the machine, getting boiled and treated. A few minutes later I took a long taste of the end result: a glass of delicious drinking water.*
>
> *The occasion was a tour of a facility that burns human waste and produces water and electricity (plus a little ash). . . .*
>
> *The water tasted as good as any I've had out of a bottle. And having studied the engineering behind it, I would happily drink it every day. It's that safe.*
>
> Source: Bill Gates. "This Ingenious Machine Turns Feces into Drinking Water." *Gates Notes*. Gates Notes, January 5, 2015. Web. Accessed October 1, 2018.

Changing Minds

The writer shares his opinion that drinking water from the new toilet isn't harmful. Do you think you would drink the water? Why or why not? Use facts to explain your answer. Try to convince a friend with an opposite opinion.

CHAPTER
FIVE

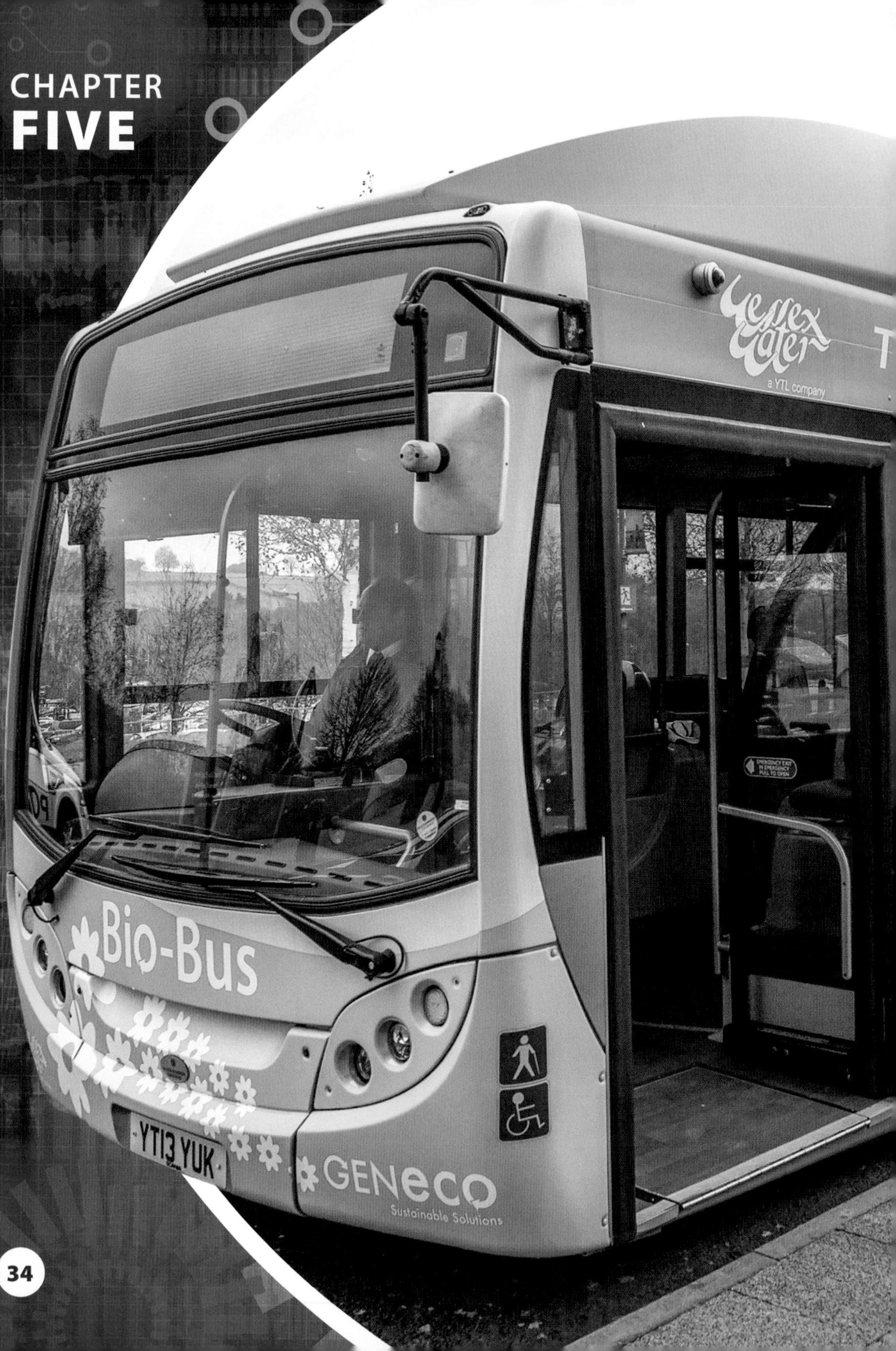

THE POWER OF POO

Global warming is a major problem. Many cities around the world are looking for new ways to combat climate change. Poop might be an answer.

Some cities are using poop to power vehicles. One shining example is what many people have started calling the poo bus. In 2014, a line of poo-powered buses was created in Bristol, United Kingdom. They ran on biogas created from a combination of sewage and food scraps.

The buses can travel approximately 190 miles (300 km) on a full tank. They produce

The official name for the poo bus is the Bio-Bus.

20 to 30 percent less carbon dioxide than buses that run on diesel. Replacing diesel fuel also cuts back on air pollution by 97 percent.

DYNAMIC DOGGY DOO-DOO

Brian Harper isn't the only one thinking about using dog poo for fuel. In 2018, Waterloo in Ontario, Canada, did an experiment. Local politicians there built concrete storage containers in three city parks. Dog walkers were told to drop their doggy discards into these bins. The dog poo was collected separately from the trash. It was taken to a treatment plant. The biomethane gas produced was used to create electricity for the town. During the first five months, the poop created enough electricity to power 13 homes.

FROM STOOL TO FUEL

In January 2018, an inventor in the United Kingdom named Brian Harper made global headlines. He took the idea of using poop for power one step further. He created a streetlight that runs on doggy doo.

The lamppost's design isn't

In 2010, Matthew Mazzotta also designed a poop-powered lamppost.

Some museums have exhibits where people can learn about using poop and other biofuels as energy.

complicated. At the bottom of the lamppost is a compartment. Dog walkers put the poop into the compartment and close the door. Then they turn a handle.

The lamppost works like an anaerobic digester. It breaks down dog doo and produces biogas that fuels the light. Harper says ten bags of poo will power the light for two hours. The lamppost is environmentally friendly and keeps the ground clean.

POO-POWERED PHONES

Perhaps the most surprising idea is using poo-power for smartphones and other electronic devices. In November 2014, a scientific study was published. Researchers discovered a natural process that happens inside poop.

The study was based on a simple concept. Human and animal waste contain bacteria. Under the right conditions, the bacteria feed off of iron minerals in the poop. When this happens, an electrical charge is

FUN FACTS ABOUT POOP!

Poop is about 75 percent water. The other 25 percent is solid waste. The average person produces approximately 700 pounds (320 kg) of poop per year. That weighs about as much as a large motorcycle. The flush toilet was invented in 1596. It didn't become popular until 1851. One person's daily poop can generate enough electricity to power a 60-watt light bulb for nine hours.

released into the air. This charge can be captured and used for power. The amount of electricity would be enough to power a phone battery.

As of 2018, the world's first working poop-powered phone hasn't become widely available. Neither has the doggy-doo lamppost. They're still in the early stages of development. But scientists are experimenting with ways to make these ideas possible. In the meantime, they are collaborating with farmers, sanitation plants, and city governments all over the world. They are working together to make poop power a dependable reality.

STRAIGHT TO THE
SOURCE

William Simmons Jr. works for a company that develops waste-to-energy programs. In 2015, he was asked in an interview why waste power wasn't more popular in the United States:

> *A great opportunity exists to create partnerships that increase the efficient use of existing waste management infrastructure used by industry, cities, towns, and states while providing economic opportunities for farmers and organic waste managers. If it is organic, it has energy potential. . . . The U.S. should embrace the tremendous resources we have available "above the dirt" in the form of organic wastes, and work to develop more innovative, financially attractive ways of repurposing these materials from a "waste" into a "resource."*

> Source: Megan Greenwalt. "High Costs Prevent Wide Adoption of Animal Waste-to-Energy Systems." *Waste 360*. Informa, February 25, 2015. Web. Accessed October 1, 2018.

Point of View

The writer views using poop for power in a very favorable way. Why does he think it's such a good idea? Do you agree? Why or why not? Use examples to support your argument.

FAST FACTS

- Burning fossil fuels is the largest source of carbon dioxide emissions.

- Since the 1800s, Earth's average temperature has risen about 1.62 degrees Fahrenheit (0.9°C).

- Farm animal manure causes 14.5 percent of annual global greenhouse gas emissions.

- Approximately 60 percent of the global population doesn't have a home toilet.

- Approximately 1.8 billion people worldwide drink water from a source that may contain poop.

- There are more than 253 working anaerobic digesters on US farms. In 2017, these digesters reduced greenhouse gas emissions by 4.35 million short tons (3.95 million metric tons).

- The United States has approximately 2,200 working biogas systems across all 50 states. Adding 13,500 new systems would be like cutting back on the emissions of up to 11 million cars.

- The average person produces about 700 pounds (320 kg) of poop per year. One person's daily poop can generate enough electricity to power a 60-watt light bulb for nine hours.

STOP AND
THINK

Why Do I Care?

Maybe you live in a house with plenty of working toilets. But that doesn't mean you can't think about the ways other people live. Chapter Four states that 60 percent of people around the world don't have toilets in their home. Do you take things like running water or an indoor bathroom for granted? How might your life be different if you didn't have a working toilet in your house to use?

Another View

This book explains some of the ways in which poop can be used to create power. It also explains why this process can help curb global warming. As you know, every source is different. Ask a librarian or another adult to help you find another source that discusses why using poop for power is either favorable or unfavorable. Write a short essay comparing and contrasting the new source's point of view with that of this book's author. What is the point of view of each author? How are they similar and why? How are they different and why?

Say What?

Studying the many ways in which poop can be used as a renewable energy source can mean learning a lot of new vocabulary. Find five words in this book you've never heard before. Use a dictionary to find out what they mean. Then write the meanings in your own words, and use each word in a new sentence.

Surprise Me

After reading this book, what two or three facts about the process of converting poop to power did you find most surprising? Write a few sentences about each fact. Why did you find each fact surprising?

GLOSSARY

algae
a family of simple, nonflowering organisms

bacteria
single-celled microorganisms, some of which can cause diseases

biological
having to do with living things and processes

biomethane
a purified form of biogas that can be used as natural gas

fertilizer
a mixture of healthy materials, which can include poop, that are added to make soil produce more plants

greenhouse gas
a type of gas that traps heat in the atmosphere and contributes to global warming

microorganisms
living things that can't be seen without a microscope

nutrient
something in food that helps people, animals, and plants live and grow

sanitation
the promotion of community health standards and disease prevention, especially by keeping up sewage systems

sustainable
able to be maintained at a certain rate or level

ONLINE
RESOURCES

To learn more about turning poop into power, visit our free resource websites below.

Visit **abdocorelibrary.com** or scan this QR code for free Common Core resources for teachers and students, including vetted activities, multimedia, and booklinks, for deeper subject comprehension.

Visit **abdobooklinks.com** or scan this QR code for free additional online weblinks for further learning. These links are routinely monitored and updated to provide the most current information available.

LEARN
MORE

Conley, Kate. *Biofuels*. Minneapolis, MN: Abdo Publishing, 2017. Print.

Woolf, Alex. *You Wouldn't Want to Live Without Poop!* New York: Franklin Watts, 2016. Print.

INDEX

About the Author

Alexis Burling has written more than 25 nonfiction books for young readers. She is also a book critic with reviews published in the *New York Times*, *San Francisco Chronicle*, and other publications. She lives with her husband in the Pacific Northwest.